NIKIFOROS VRETTAKOS

Selected Poems

NIKIFOROS VRETTAKOS

Selected Poems

Translated by
David Connolly

AIORA

David Connolly is Professor of Translation Studies at the Aristotle University of Thessaloniki. He has translated over 40 books with works by contemporary Greek writers. His translations have received prizes in the USA, the UK and Greece.

ACKNOWLEDGEMENTS: A number of the poems contained in this volume were first published in earlier versions in *Greek Letters, A Journal of Modern Greek Literature in Translation* and *The Charioteer, An Annual Review of Modern Greek Culture*.

© Aiora Press 2015

All rights reserved. No part of this publication may be reproduced, stored in a retrieval system, or transmitted, in any form or by any means, electronic, mechanical, photocopying, recording or otherwise, without written permission of the publishers.

ISBN: 978-618-5048-30-3

AIORA PRESS
11 Mavromichali st.
Athens 10679 - Greece
tel: +30 210 3839000
www.aiora.gr

Contents

Introduction 11

Poems
   From: THE DISTINGUISHED PLANET (1983)
      Vanity 25
      Reckoning 27
      Apologia to a Mountain 29
      The Great Work 31
      The Difficult Mountain 33
   From: SUNLAMP (1984)
      My Writing 35
      The Landscape's Transformation 37
      Translation 39
      Hospitality 41
      Transfusion 43
   From: GIFTS IN ABEYANCE (1986)
      Whatever Happens 45
      A Song for the Earth 47
      A Little Song 49
      A Different Soldier 51
      The Field of Words 53

Treeplanting	55
The Idea of Departing	57
The Ark	59
The Destruction of Faces	61
The Contest and the Adjudicator	63
My Monogram	65

From: CHOIR (1988)

Poems for the Same Mountain V	67
Poems for the Same Mountain X	69
Creation	71
Poetry	73

From: THE PHILOSOPHY OF FLOWERS (1990)

The Pulse	75
Manifest Evidence	77
I've Spoken	79
Seminar	81
Creation	83

From: ENCOUNTER WITH THE SEA (1991)

As If At Times You'd Ceased...	85
My Gaze...	87
The Constant Dream...	89
I'd Gone...	91
Other Waves...	93
I Pondered Much...	95
Poetry...	97
Beside My Other...	99

Chronology	101
Book-length English Translations	105
Index of Greek Titles	107

*Poetry is but a magnifying glass to reality.
The magnification of the true dimensions
of man and of the world which surrounds us
can convey to us a sense of the splendour
of the life we are ready to destroy.*

N.V.

Introduction

"TRANSLATING" THE POETRY OF NIKIFOROS VRETTAKOS

One of the multiple meanings of the verb "to translate" is "to transfer (the body or the relics of a saint) from one resting place to another."[1] Without in any way wishing to canonize Nikiforos Vrettakos, I will use the term in this sense in order to examine the corpus of his work. What is it that the "translator" should take care to transfer to another (linguistic and cultural) resting place? I do not intend here to discuss the actual process of translating, in other words the *how*, but rather I will focus on what constitutes the essence of his poetical work. What has remained of his poetical work today, almost twenty-five years after his death? For, as he himself aptly noted: 'The present passes all too quickly; the future is long. The important thing is what we leave behind us."[2]

It is the fate of most Greek poets to be forgotten following their death. Even in the case of major poets, the interest of

---

1. *Collins English Dictionary*, Glasgow: HarperCollins Publishers, ⁴1998.
2. Interview with G. Sarigiannis, in the newspaper *Ta Nea* (03/03/1987), p. 25.

the reading public tends to wane before these poets eventually take their due place in the literary pantheon. And in the majority of cases, they remain with a somewhat superficial label stemming from a cursory reading of their work. So, for example, Yannis Ritsos is often referred to as the "poet of Greekness", Odysseus Elytis as the "poet of the Aegean" and Nikiforos Vrettakos as the "poet of love and peace". Usually, and as might be expected, the poets themselves are not particularly fond of such labels. It would seem, however, that Vrettakos was not at all upset by his label.[3] However, in any attempt to "translate" Vrettakos in the sense I previously mentioned, would it be sufficient simply to transfer these few characteristics? Presumably not. So what are the essential characteristics of his work that constitute his poetic legacy and that the translator is required to transfer?

Noticeable in all the works from the last decade of his life is a distinct endeavour on the part of the poet to settle his poetic accounts through poetry itself. In fact, the poems from this period constitute something of an epilogue to his entire poetic work and encapsulate the very essence of his poetry that his aspiring "translator" must locate and transfer. They are characterized by a sense of imminent departure, a feeling of indebtedness to the world around him and a need to bid farewell to his friends-symbols: the light, the sun, his beloved mount Taygetus, the trees, the flowers, the sea, the hallowed Christ-like figure of man, but also to poetry itself. The same tone can be observed in all the collections of this last period:

---

[3]. See interview with Sarandos Sakellakos, in the magazine *ENA* (04/09/1991), p. 78-82.

The Distinguished Planet (1983), *The Sun's Lamp* (1984), *Gifts in Abeyance* (1986), *Choir* (1988), *The Philosophy of Flowers* (1988) and is particularly well exemplified in "Epilogue", the last poem in his last collection, *Encounter with the Sea* (1991)[4]:

EPILOGUE

You might expect, dear sea, before
I desert your shore, to hear
my last few hoary words:
"Goodnight", "It is accomplished."
But no, I won't utter them to each of you
separately, but to all of you together:
to the man, dear sea, who walked
upon you, to the sun, to you,
to the mountains, to the flowers, to the whole
of my beloved World here around me.

I'll bid my farewell tomorrow, the next day,
I can't be sure, to Poetry alone. For
poetry was all of you together.

I am not going to attempt a literary analysis of these symbols. As an aspiring "translator" of his work, it is sufficient for me to simply identify and (re-)locate them because it is these that constitute the essence or *bones* of his poetic corpus. "In my endeavour to say what I wanted," he explains, "I collected the symbols necessary for my sensitivity and my aims. And on

---

4. I have not included in this list the collections *Sicilian Poems* (1990) and *Protest* (1991) as the poems they contain were written before 1981 and from the point of view of both theme and tone belong to an earlier period.

the whole I took these elements from the Greek landscape."[5] There are two things I wish to point out concerning his symbols or, as I refer to them here, the bones of his poetry, since both are directly connected with any "translation" of his work. The first concerns the universality of his symbols and, by extension, of his poetic message. His poems are deeply rooted in the Greek landscape and coloured by the Greek light, but their themes are ecumenical. The two basic axes of his poetry (the "two hemispheres", as he himself called them) are nature and man: an almost mystical intoxication with the beauty of creation yet, at the same time, a deep sense of grief for the fate of the most wonderful creation, man. The role of the poet, however, is not only to observe and describe the beauty of the world or the suffering of man. Poetry for Vrettakos is also a sacred mission as he explains in a poem from *Gifts in Abeyance*:

THE TEN COMMANDMENTS

I minister to life's suffering, yet I
mustn't forget that I was also born
a high priest of beauty and I'm obliged
to celebrate our world, to transform
its radiance into the written word.
       The First
and Last Commandment
of beauty: love.

And there are innumerable poems in which the poet pro-

---

5. Interview with Elena Houzouri, in the newspaper *Rizospastis* (29/06/1980), p. 4.

claims love as that which bridges the void between the world's beauty and man's suffering and in which love is presented, more generally, as a unifying element in the world. So much so that we are justified in taking love to be the main message of his poetry, as being that essential element of his poetic corpus that we are attempting to identify and (re-)locate. Vrettakos confirms this in a more poetic way: "My tiny monogram / on my memorial stone: love" (The Monogram). There is no need to expand on this. I simply note the universality of this message; the truly universal pulse of the body of his poetry. So the translator's first concern in transferring this body should be to retain its universal message, its essential theme of love.

The beauty of the physical world, the anthropocentric nature of his poetry (a term he himself accepted[6]), the message of love: simple things. Some would say *simplistic*. Vrettakos gives his own answer to this characterization: "Unfortunately there are times when one becomes simplistic just by speaking the truth".[7] And here I wish to make a second point concerning the message of his poetry, the bones, that is, of his poetic work. What saves his message from being simplistic is the sincerity of his poetic voice ("I am what I write, I am my face," he said). And together with the sincerity of his poetic voice is his inner need for poetic expression. No poem by Vrettakos gives the impression that it was written simply in order to be

---

6. See interview with Elena Houzouri, in the newspaper *Rizospastis* (29/06/1980), p. 4.
7. Nikiforos Vrettakos, *Poietikos logos ke ethniki alitheia*, Athens 1988, p. 19.

written, that it is, in other words, the product of the poetic workshop. There is nothing affected or pretentious in his poetry. "Writing is a personal need. A need of existence itself... Writing for me means life,"[8] he says, and elsewhere he explains: "I lived by writing. I don't mean writing was a livelihood, rather it was a biological need [...]. Those worlds of sentiments that accumulate inside me would have killed me if I hadn't written."[9]

But a poem is not only its subject matter just as a body is not only its bones, even though in many translations it is, unfortunately, only the bones of a poetic work that are transferred. Bones require flesh and subject matter requires poetic expression. Again, however, I am not going to attempt a literary analysis of Vrettakos's language or poetic technique. As a "translator", I am still looking for the quiddity of his poetic corpus. What, then, is that particular characteristic of his language that has to be transferred together with his message?

Apart from the undisputed fact that he was one of the most genuine and gifted lyrical voices of his generation, what characterizes his poetic voice is the simplicity of its expression. It is a poetic voice that, as has been noted, "surprises with its 'simplicity'"[10], but also with its sufficiency and succinctness I might add. And just as the simplicity of his mes-

---

8. Interview with Giorgos Pilichos, in the newspaper *Ta Nea* (06/12/1982), p. 7.
9. Interview with G. Sarigiannis, in the newspaper *Ta Nea* (03/03/1987), p. 25.
10. Vicenzo Rotolo, "Mythos ke pragmatikotita. I Poiesi tou Nikiforou Vrettakou", in *Aiolika Grammata* 115-116 (May-August 1990), p. 39.

sage does not mean simplism, so also the simplicity of his expression does not mean a lack of creative imagination or of linguistic inventiveness. On the contrary, it is the result of a conscious effort on the part of the poet to make his message understandable and his voice accessible. It is, as Vincenzo Rotolo observes, "a complete identification of world view and language",[11] a complete identification, that is, of message and expression. Vrettakos himself says in connection with this: "I tried first and foremost to maintain clarity in my writing [...]. We must not forget that we are talking to another person. Of course, it's extremely difficult to arrive at perfection with regard to simplicity of expression."[12] Extremely difficult indeed, yet something Vrettakos manages not because of any innate facility, but through toil and exhaustive reworking of his material. It is an elaborate and finely-wrought simplicity. And just as it is love that constitutes the essence of his poetic message, so, too, in the expression of this message, it is love once again that constitutes the key. As Vrettakos puts it: "the golden key to simplicity / in speaking to all the creatures / round about us is provided by love". The translator's second concern, then, when transferring Vrettakos's work should be to retain the simplicity of his linguistic expression.

There is still something missing, however, from the body we wish to "translate": that which beyond bones and flesh gives

---

11. Op. cit., p. 39.
12. Interview with Elena Houzouri, in the newspaper *Rizospastis* (29/06/1980), p. 4.

it life. Its blood, that is. And we might ask, where is the blood in a poetic work? I am being in no way original when I say that a poem's blood is the sentiment it conveys. Vrettakos refers to this fact when he writes: "So much blood ran from within me. / Thousands upon thousands of sheets of paper / became soaked on my table" (Reckoning) and "The notes rise up in my soul and in my blood" (A Song For the Earth). His subject matter may be simple, his linguistic expression simple, but the sentiment contained in his poems imbues them with extraordinary power and effectiveness. His poetry is in-

Translator and poet, Sparta, July 20 1991.

fused with sentiment (his blood, or soul as he sometimes refers to it), instilling it with a strong emotional charge. So much so that it often verges on sentimentalism, but never lapses into this. Just as the simplicity of his message is saved from becoming simplicity by the sincerity of his voice, so also the sentiment in his poetry is saved from becoming sentimentality by the purity of his emotion. His poetry wells up from his own soul so that each word is imbued with his characteristic virtues of kindness, humility, innocence and love on the one hand and, on the other, with the grief and indignation he feels at the injustice he observes in the world. He has said that he never wrote a word that hadn't passed through him because what is about to be born, by passing through us, is fuelled by our own soul. Without a part of the soul, he says, poetry doesn't exist; it has to be charged with the human soul. And for this reason it is perpetuated, becoming a part of life that time can never eradicate.[13] Impregnated, therefore, with his own blood (or soul), words lose their conventional, everyday meanings and are transubstantiated so that they emit light and life as he describes in the following poem from *Gifts in Abeyance*:

PREPARATION

Once again flames flit about
inside me, seeking an outlet. They are
words that are consumed, that lose
their terrestrial weight, take on

---

13. T.V. interview with Nikos Dimou, "I peripeteia enos poiematos", ET2 1989.

the attributes of the sun
and become poetry.

The translator's third concern, then, in the transfer of Vrettakos's poetical body is to ensure its emotional charge is retained.

These are the three essential elements, then, that should concern his aspiring "translator": his universal message, the simplicity of his linguistic expression and the sentiment of his verse. But the question still remains: why should we translate Vrettakos, transferring the body of his work to another (linguistic and cultural) resting place? Firstly, I think, because his subject matter (the *bones* of his poetry): love, peace, suffering, wonder and respect for the physical environment is ecumenical and remains relevant today more than ever. These are topics that find their response in the deepest roots of human nature and, truly, constitute the bones of human existence. Secondly, because simplicity of expression (the *flesh* of his poetry) constitutes a welcome oasis in the field of poetry, particularly in the post-modern world to which we have become accustomed. Vrettakos never forgot that through his poetry he was communicating with others and he respected his readers, whereas often when reading poetry today, the reader feels that he is more an eavesdropper or a surreptitious reader of the personal confession of a stranger who doesn't even take him into account. And thirdly, because in much art today, sentiment (the *blood* in his poetry) is left aside in favour of a sterile intellectualism, though in poetry, at least, it is sentiment and not argumentation that convinces the reader. In speaking of much contemporary poetry, Vrettakos himself remarked: "people don't read poetry, because poetry doesn't grip them. It doesn't contain any emotion, which is the substratum of life".[14]

I began this short introduction to Vrettakos's work by examining it from the point of view of the translator and using one of the many meanings of the verb "to translate" in order to present what, in my view, are three of its essential characteristics. I hope it has become clear that, characterized as it is by simplicity and lucidity and rich in sentiment, Vrettakos's poetry requires little analysis or explanation. As such, any lengthy introduction would only render a disservice to a poet who wanted his poetry to be "a flowering branch within everyone's reach".

David Connolly
Athens, 2015

---

14. Interview in the newspaper *Ta Nea* (02/02/1982).

Selected Poems

Από τη συλλογή *Ὁ Διακεκριμένος Πλανήτης*

ΜΑΤΑΙΟΔΟΞΙΑ

Ἀκόμη δέν ἔφυγα ἀπό μένα. Μιλῶ ὧρες-ὧρες
ὡς νά εἶμαι ὁ κυρίαρχος ἑνός κόσμου
ὅπου οἱ ἄλλοι δέν ἔχουνε τίποτα. Ὡς νά εἶμαι
ἕνας κύριος ἐνταλμένος νά λέει: «Ἐγώ».
Τό εἶχα εἰπεῖ ἀλλ' ἀκόμη δέν ἔγινα ὅπως ἕνα λουλούδι
μετέχον καί ἀμέτοχο, μέ μόνο δικό του
τήν ἄκρη τῆς πέτρας πού φύτρωσε πάνω της.

From: *The Distinguished Planet*

VANITY

I still haven't got away from me. At times I talk
as if I am the master of a world
in which others have nothing. As if I am
a ruler charged to say: "I".
Though I said it I still haven't become like a flower
part and apart, with just one thing its own
the edge of the rock where it sprouted.

ΑΠΟΛΟΓΙΣΜΟΣ

Ἔτρεξεν αἷμα πολύ ἀπό μέσα μου.
Μυριάδες μυριάδων φύλλα χαρτιοῦ
ποτιστήκανε στό τραπέζι μου.
Μουσκεμένα ὥς τίς μέσα ἶνες τους, ὅσους
ἀνέμους κι ἄν κάνει δέν θά στεγνώσουνε.
Φέρνοντάς τα ὁ ἐπίγονος στ' αὐτί του
θ' ἀκούει μέσα τους ἕνα θρόϊσμα
θαλάσσης ἤ φυλλωσιᾶς, ἁπαλό, συνεχές,
ἀνεξάντλητο: τό αἷμα μου.

RECKONING

So much blood ran from within me.
Thousands upon thousands of sheets of paper
became soaked on my table.
Saturated to their innermost fibres, they
won't dry however many winds blow.
Putting them to his ear some descendant
will hear within them a whispering
of sea or foliage, soft, constant,
inexhaustible: my blood.

ΑΠΟΛΟΓΟΣ Σ' ΕΝΑ ΒΟΥΝΟ

Προνόμιο ἄλλο δέν ἀξιώνω ἐκτός ἀπ' τήν ὕπαρξη.
Ἔχω ἀποχτήσει τόν πλοῦτο νά εἶμαι
ἤδη μιά πέτρα, ψυχρή πρός τή ματαιότητα,
εὐαίσθητη πρός τό φῶς. Δέν μοῦ καίει τό χιόνι
τήν πανάρχαιη γυμνότητα. Ἀρθρώνω
τό λόγο μου, ὅπως ἐσύ τούς χειμάρρους σου, ἤ
τούς ἀχούς τῶν δασῶν σου. Δέ μέ διακόπτουν
οἱ θύελλες ἤ τό σκοτάδι. Κι ὅταν δέν βλέπω
ἀκούω τόν ἥλιο, ἤ τῆς Ἀφροδίτης
τό ἁμάξι καθώς διαπλέει τά διάφανα
οὐράνια μαρμαίροντας. Συγκέντρωσα
μέσα μου τ' ἀναγκαῖα, ἐξασφάλισα
ὅ,τι μοῦ χρειάζεται. Εὐτύχησα.

APOLOGIA TO A MOUNTAIN

I claim no privilege other than existence.
I've acquired the wealth to be
already a rock, indifferent to vanity,
sensitive to light. The snow can't sear
my age-old nakedness. I articulate
my words as you do your torrents, or
the whispers of your forests. Neither storm
nor darkness stops me. And when I don't see
the sun I hear it, or Aphrodite's
chariot as glittering it sails through
the translucent heavens. I've gathered
the necessities within me, I've secured
all I need. I'm content.

ΤΟ ΜΕΓΑΛΟ ΕΡΓΟ

Κοιτάζοντας τή μηλιά
πού φύτεψα σήμερα,
συλλογίζομαι πώς
μεγαλύτερο ἔργο
δέν ὑπάρχει ἀπό τό
νά κάνει κανείς
τό χῶμα λουλούδια.

Κι ὅταν κάνω σιωπή,
σταματώντας νά σκέφτομαι,
ἀκούω κοντά μου
τό μεγάλο μου γείτονα.

(Μέσα στίς μῆτρες
ὅλων τῶν δέντρων μου
ρέει ὁ Θεός).

THE GREAT WORK

Gazing at the apple tree
that I planted today,
I reflect that
no greater work
exists
than turning
the earth into flowers.

And when I fall silent,
ceasing to think,
nearby me I hear
my great neighbour.

(Flowing in the wombs
of all my trees
is God).

ΤΟ ΔΥΣΚΟΛΟ ΟΡΟΣ

Πῆρε τούς μαθητές του ὁ Ἰησοῦς κι ἀνηφόρισε
στό δύσκολο Ὄρος, στήν κορφή του ὅπου εἶναι
μόνος κανείς, σέ σύννεφα ἀνάμεσα καί σέ ἀνέμους.
Καί εἶπε, χωρίς νά ξέρει ἄν ἀκούγεται:
«Ἡ ἀγάπη εἶναι ἀλήθεια κ' ἡ ἀλήθεια ἀγάπη».
Καί τό ὅτι κανείς δέν κατάλαβε τίποτε
τό εἶδε στά πρόσωπα τῶν μαθητῶν του
πού κοιταζόντουσαν. Νιώθοντας μόνος
ἀνάμεσα στό κενό καί τό ψύχος,
ἔμεινε ἀκίνητος ὡς νά μαρμάρωσε
καί βυθίστη σέ συλλογή: «Γιά πόσον καιρό;»
Καί βλέποντας κάτω τή θάλασσα,
ταράχτηκε σφόδρα: «Ὥσπου τό πλήρωμα
νά ρθεῖ τῆς ἀγάπης, μπορεῖ νά χρειαστοῦν
τόσα δάκρυα ὅσα εἶναι ὅλες οἱ θάλασσες».

Καί ξεκίνησε ἔπειτα, ἔτσι ὅπως ἤτανε,
γιά τούς αἰῶνες. Μετακινιόταν τό Ὄρος,
μέ αὐτόν στήν κορφή, διπλωμένον στά σύννεφα.

THE DIFFICULT MOUNT

Taking his disciples Jesus ascended
the difficult Mount, to its summit where
one is alone, amid clouds and winds.
And, without knowing if any could hear, he said:
"Love is truth and truth love".
And that no one understood anything
he saw in the faces of his disciples
who stared at each other.
                        Feeling alone
between the void and the chill,
he remained still as if turned to stone
and sank into thought: "How much longer?"
And seeing the sea below,
he was deeply shaken: "Till the fullness
of love comes, it may take
as many tears as are in all the seas".

And then he set out, just as he was,
through the centuries. The Mount moved
with him on its summit, enveloped in clouds.

Από τη συλλογή *Ηλιακός Λύχνος*

Η ΓΡΑΦΗ ΜΟΥ

Έμαθα γραφή καί ἀνάγνωση (πρίν
ἀπό τή γραφή καί πρίν ἀπό τήν ἀνάγνωση)
γιά νά γράψω τή μέρα, τή νύχτα, τό φῶς,
προπαντός τούς πολύχρωμους ἐκείνους ψιθύρους
πού βρίσκονται μέσα μου. Νά γράψω
τή γλώσσα τῶν λυγμῶν πού εἶναι μία
σ' ὅλο τόν κόσμο. Τίς μητέρες - Μαρίες
πού ἄν ξεκινούσανε ὅλες μαζί,
ἡ μαύρη πομπή τους θά σχημάτιζε
ζώνη γύρω ἀπ' τή γῆς.
　　　　Ὅλες τοῦτες
οἱ πέτρες πού βρίσκονται γύρω μου
εἶναι πλάκες τοῦ Θεοῦ ὅπου πάνω τους,
ἔμαθα γραφή καί ἀνάγνωση,
νά γράψω μέ μιά κιμωλία τήν ἀγάπη.

From: *Sunlamp*

MY WRITING

I learned reading and writing (even
before reading and before writing)
so I might write the day, the night, the light,
above all those multicoloured whispers
contained within me. So I might write
the language of tears which is one
the world over. Write the mothers Mary
whose sombre procession, were they all
to set out together, would form
a ring round the earth.
                      All these
rocks lying round about me
are God's slates on which
I learned reading and writing,
how using chalk to write love.

Η ΜΕΤΑΜΟΡΦΩΣΗ ΤΟΥ ΤΟΠΙΟΥ

Ἡ παρουσία σου ἄλλαξε ξαφνικά τή μορφή,
τό ρυθμό, τήν ἀπόχρωση τοῦ τοπίου.
Φωστιστῆκαν τά δέντρα, τά οὐράνια διευρύνθηκαν,
ὁ ὁρίζοντας βάθυνε, ἀναδείχτηκαν τά βουνά.
Εἶναι τόση ἡ διαφάνεια πού ἀκόμη καί μέσα μου
δέν κρύβεται τίποτα. Ἄν προσέξεις θά δεῖς
νά σαλεύουνε ὅπως ἕνας ἀπέραντος ἀγρός
ἀπό στάχυα, τ' ἄγραφά μου ποιήματα.

THE LANDSCAPE'S TRANSFORMATION

Your presence suddenly changed the shape,
rhythm, hue of the landscape.
The trees were brightened, the heavens widened,
the horizon deepened, the mountains stood out.
The clarity is such that even within me
nothing is concealed. If you look carefully you'll see
swaying like a vast field
of corn, my unwritten poems.

Η ΜΕΤΑΦΡΑΣΗ

Συναναστράφηκα τά ἔμψυχα, τά ἄψυχα, ὅλα
ὅσα φτάνει τό χέρι, τό βλέμμα, ἡ αἴσθηση
πού δέν ἔχει ὄργανο στό ἀνθρώπινο πρόσωπο.
Τά πλησίασα ὅσο μποροῦσε νά γίνει
πιό πολύ, καί τά ἄκουσα. Διαλογίστηκα
ἄν μεταφράζονται οἱ γλῶσσες τους
καί προσπάθησα. Φθόγγος πρός λέξη,
προτάσεις σιωπῆς, σῆμα πρός λέξη,
ὅσο πού τίς ἀπόδωσα τέλος, μέ μιά
μόνο λέξη. Τίς ὀνόμασα φῶς.

TRANSLATION

I mixed with things animate and inanimate, everything
within reach of touch, sight and the sense
that has no organ on the human face.
I came as close to them as was practically
possible, and I listened to them. I pondered
whether their languages are translatable
and I tried. Sound into word,
sentences of silence, sign into word,
till eventually I rendered them, with just
one word. I called them light.

Η ΦΙΛΟΞΕΝΙΑ

Γίνεται κάποτε νά καλύπτει ὁ ἕνας ἄνθρωπος
τόν ἄλλον μέ φῶς. Εἶναι τό βλέμμα
τῆς ἀγάπης πού ἔχει τήν ἀρχή του στό ἄπειρο.

Σχημάτιζε πάνω μου μιά σκέπη
τό βλέμμα σου μέ κάτι κλαδιά φωτεινά,
ἀπροσδιόριστα. (Δέν ἔβρισκε τρόπο,
θυρίδα νά μπεῖ, ὁ ἀέρας πού φύσαγε).
Τόσο, πού φεύγοντας, ἔνιωθα ἔπειτα
τήν ἀνάγκη νά εἰπῶ, ἄν ὄχι μέ λέξεις,
μ' ἕνα χαμόγελο, ἄϋλο σχεδόν:

               «Εὐχαριστῶ
τό βλέμμα σου γιά τή φιλοξενία».

HOSPITALITY

Sometimes it happens that one person covers
another with light. It's the look
of love that has its beginning in infinity.

Your look formed a roof over me
with branches that were bright,
indefinable. (There was no way,
no nook for the wind blowing to enter).
So much so that, on leaving, I felt
the need to say, if not in words,
with a smile, incorporeal almost:

                "I'm grateful
to your look for the hospitality".

ΜΕΤΑΓΓΙΣΗ

Μέ τά μάτια τῶν ἄλλων μᾶς βλέπει
ὁ Θεός, μεταγγίζοντας μέσα μας κάτι
ἀπ' τό πλῆρες του ἄγνωστο φῶς. Κι αὐτή
ἡ μετάγγιση πού λαβαίνω ἀπ' τό βλέμμα σου
εἶναι ἀνεξάντλητη. Κάθε φορά
αἰσθάνομαι σάμπως νά μήν περιέχει
τίποτε ἄλλο τό σῶμα μου. Ἕνα δέντρο
ἀνθισμένο μέ γιομίζει ὁλόκληρο.

TRANSFUSION

It's through the eyes of others that God
sees us, transfusing into us something
of his replete unknown light. And this
transfusion that I receive from your gaze
is inexhaustible. Each time
I feel as though my body
contains nothing else. A tree
in bloom fills me entirely.

Από τη συλλογή *Εκκρεμής δωρεά*

Ο,ΤΙ ΚΑΙ ΝΑ ΣΥΜΒΕΙ

Ὅ,τι καί νά συμβεῖ, δέν θά τόν ἀρνηθῶ
τόν κόσμο. Κι ἄν μοῦ κόψουν τά χέρια
καί δέν ἔχω ἀγκάλη, θά μπορῶ
ν' ἀκουμπῶ τό μέτωπό μου στό δέντρο,
τό μέτωπό μου στήν πέτρα, τό δαρμένο
ἀπ' τήν ἔρημο μάγουλό μου στό φῶς.

From: *Gifts in Abeyance*

WHATEVER HAPPENS

Whatever happens, I won't reject
the world. Even if they cut off my arms
so I can't embrace it, I'll still be able
to rest my brow against a tree,
my brow against a rock, my cheek
wizened by the wilderness against the light.

ΕΝΑ ΑΣΜΑ ΓΙΑ ΤΗ ΓΗ

Θά μπορούσα νά γράψω ἕνα ἄσμα ἀσμάτων
γιά τό ἀστέρι τῶν ἀστεριῶν, πού θά ἐκάλυπτε
ὅλες τίς μορφές τῆς ζωῆς, ἔμψυχα, ἄψυχα.
Γιατί καί τά ἄψυχα εἶναι ζωή. Ἔχω
μέσα μου ἕτοιμη ὅλη τή μουσική,
κλίμακες, τόνους, χρώματα ἤχων
πού ἄλλοτε ποτέ δέν ἀκούστηκαν.

Κάποτε μάλιστα ἰδίως τήν ὥρα
πού βλέπω τόν ἥλιο ν' ἀνατέλλει
προβάλλοντας στήν ἄκρη τοῦ ὁρίζοντα,
θαρρῶ πώς ἀκούγομαι ἀπ' ὅλα
τά γύρω μου.
      (Ἀναβράζουν
οἱ φθόγγοι στήν ψυχή καί στό αἷμα μου).

A SONG FOR THE EARTH

I could compose a song of songs
about the star of stars, which would include
all forms of life, animate and inanimate.
For inanimate things are life too. I have
all the music ready inside me,
scales, tones, timbres of sound
never heard before.

And sometimes, especially when
I watch the sun rising
appearing at the horizon's edge,
I feel as if I'm heard by everything
round about me.
         (The notes
rise up in my soul and in my blood.)

ΜΙΚΡΗ ΩΔΗ

Καθισμένος ἀντίκρυ στό καλό μου
βουνό, θεωρῶ καί στοχάζομαι. Ὡραῖοι
συνειρμοί χρωμάτων, πραγμάτων
ὁ κόσμος μας. Ἐντέλεια καί φῶς.
Καί λέω πώς θά 'πρεπε νά μήν
κατοικεῖται ἀπ' τό ἔνοπλο μίσος
ἀλλά νά εἶναι ὁ κῆπος, ἡ ὡραία
ἐκκλησιά τοῦ σύμπαντος κτίσματος.
Καί μόνο ἐπισκέπτες ἀπό ἄλλους
πλανῆτες, γυμνούς ἀπό κάλλος,
νά περνοῦν γιά προσκύνημα.

A LITTLE SONG

Sitting facing my beloved
mountain, I gaze and reflect. What wonderful
associations of colours and objects
our world is. Perfection and light.
To my mind, it ought to be
not the abode of armed hate
but the garden, the beautiful
chapel in the mansion of the universe.
And only visitors from other
planets, naked in beauty,
would come in pilgrimage.

Ο ΑΛΛΟΣ ΣΤΡΑΤΙΩΤΗΣ

Θά παλέψω νά μείνω ὑπήκοος πιστός τοῦ ἀπάνω κόσμου, ὥς τό τέλος. Νά μείνω ὥς τό τέλος στρατευμένος τοῦ σύμπαντος ἐν στολῇ ἀγάπης καί ποίησης. Ν' ἀκολουθῶ, πορευόμενος, τόν ἥλιο, ὥς τό τέλος.

A DIFFERENT SOLDIER

I'll strive to remain a loyal subject
of the world above to the end; to remain
to the end in the ranks of the universe
in a uniform of love and poetry. And I'll strive,
as I go, to follow the sun to the end.

Ο ΑΓΡΟΣ ΤΩΝ ΛΕΞΕΩΝ

Ὅπως ἡ μέλισσα γύρω ἀπό ἕνα ἄγριο
λουλούδι, ὅμοια κ' ἐγώ. Τριγυρίζω
διαρκῶς γύρω ἀπ' τή λέξη.

Εὐχαριστῶ τίς μακριές σειρές
τῶν προγόνων, πού δούλεψαν τή φωνή,
τήν τεμαχίσαν σέ κρίκους, τήν κάμαν
νοήματα, τή σφυρηλάτησαν ὅπως
τό χρυσάφι οἱ μεταλλουργοί κ' ἔγινε
Ὅμηροι, Αἰσχύλοι, Εὐαγγέλια
κι ἄλλα κοσμήματα.
                Μέ τό νῆμα
τῶν λέξεων, αὐτόν τό χρυσό
τοῦ χρυσοῦ, πού βγαίνει ἀπ' τά βάθη
τῆς καρδιᾶς μου, συνδέομαι, συμμετέχω
στόν κόσμο.
      Σκεφτεῖτε:
Εἶπα καί ἔγραψα, «Ἀγαπῶ».

THE FIELD OF WORDS

Like a bee round a wild
flower, that's me. I'm constantly
hovering round the word.

I give thanks to the long lines
of ancestors, who wrought the voice,
cutting it into links, giving it
meaning, forging it as
metalworkers do gold till it became
Homer, Aeschylus, the Gospels
and other such gems.
                By the thread
of words, that gold of all
gold, which emerges from the depths
of my heart, I am linked to and share
in the world.
        Just think:
I declared and wrote, "I Love".

ΔΕΝΔΡΟΦΥΤΕΥΣΗ

Οἱ λέξεις εἶναι τό δέντρο πού πάνω του
κλαδώνεται ἡ ψυχή μου καί γίνεται ἄνθη
νά θάλλουνε στόν αἰώνα. Καρποί
γιά πεινῶντες πού ἀκόμη δέν ἔχουνε
γεννηθεῖ.
  Νιώθω εὐφροσύνη
πού φύτεψα μυγδαλιές, ἀχλαδιές
ἀλλά κι ἄλλα δέντρα, ὅπως εἶναι
αὐτά τά μικρά μου ποιήματα.

TREEPLANTING

Words are the tree on which
my soul branches, becomes blossom
flowering through the ages; fruit
for the hungry still to be
born.
      I rejoice
that I planted almond and pear trees
and other trees too, like
these little poems of mine.

Η ΙΔΕΑ ΤΗΣ ΕΞΟΔΟΥ

Εἶναι στιγμές πού νομίζω πώς ἤδη
ἔχω φύγει ἀπ' τόν κόσμο. Πώς ἀπ' ὅσα
μοῦ ἀνῆκαν καί δέν μοῦ ἀνῆκαν
πῆρα μαζί μόνον ἕνα λουλούδι
νά φωτίζω τό δρόμο μου.

Διακρίνω στό βάθος τά βουνά
σάν ἰδέες, τά δέντρα μου σάν
παιχνίδια τῆς φαντασίας. Ἀλλά,
ὅπως τρεκλίζω, μιά στό ἡμίφως
μιά στό σκοτάδι, συλλογίζομαι πώς
δέν μοῦ πάει νά μήν ὑπάρχω
καί στέκομαι. Κι ἀκόμη
πώς ἴσως εἶχα νά κάνω
κάτι περσότερο σέ τοῦτο
τόν κόσμο.
    (Μ' ἕνα λουλούδι
θά μποροῦσε κανείς νά φωτίσει
τό ἄγνωστο. Νά ρίξει σέ βάθος
λουρίδες φωτός, νά γιομίσει
διαβάσεις τήν ἄβυσσο).

THE IDEA OF DEPARTING

There are times when I feel that already
I've taken leave of the world; that of all
that was or wasn't mine
I took with me just one flower
to light my way.

In the distance, the mountains appear
like ideas, my trees like
tricks of the imagination. But
as I stumble on, now in the dimness
now in the darkness, I reflect that
non-existence is not for me
and I halt. That
perhaps I had something more
to do in this
world.
    (With one flower
it's possible to illumine
the unknown, to cast long
beams of light, to cut
passes through the abyss).

Η ΚΙΒΩΤΟΣ

Κάθε ἀνθρώπινο σῶμα, (κι αὐτό
τοῦ σκαφτιᾶ, τοῦ ψαρᾶ, τοῦ τσοπάνου,
τῆς πόρνης) εἶναι ἡ κιβωτός
τοῦ σύμπαντος μέ τά μηνύματα.

THE ARK

Every human body (including that
of the labourer, the fisherman, the shepherd
and the whore) is the ark
of the universe with its messages.

Η ΚΑΤΑΣΤΡΟΦΗ ΤΩΝ ΠΡΟΣΩΠΩΝ

Τ' ἀπωλεσμένα τους πρόσωπα τά εἶχαν ἀντικαταστήσει μέ μάσκες. Μέ ποιόν νά μιλήσει; Δέν ὑπῆρχε κανείς πίσω ἀπ' τίς μάσκες τους. Καί τότες ἐστράφη καί μιλοῦσε στόν ἥλιο, στά δέντρα, στά πράγματα· νά μή χάσει τήν ἐπαφή μέ τόν κόσμο πού εἶπε πώς εἶναι ὡραῖος.
 Νά μή σαλευθεῖ ἡ ἐγκάρδια του σχέση μέ τή γύρω του τάξη. Νά μήν κλονισθεῖ ὁ ὑπαρξιακός ἄξονάς του, ἐκεῖνο τό ὄρθιο μέσα του φῶς: ἡ Ἀγάπη.

THE DESTRUCTION OF FACES

They had replaced their lost faces
with masks. Who was he
to talk to? There was no one behind
their masks. So he began then
to talk to the sun, to the trees,
to objects; not to lose contact
with the world which he declared
was good.
        Not to derange
his loving relationship with the order
around him, not to shatter the axis
of his existence, that upright
innermost light: Love.

Η ΠΑΛΗ ΚΑΙ Ο ΕΛΛΑΝΟΔΙΚΟΣ

Πάλεψα μέ τή μοίρα σῶμα μέ σῶμα.
Προσπαθοῦσε νά μοῦ ἀφαιρέσει τό πρόσωπο.
Καί τόσο πολύ χτυπήθηκα, πού
ὅπως βάδιζα ἀκούγονταν σάν
σπασμένα γυαλιά τά κόκαλα μέσα μου.
Αὐτή τή στιγμή δέν ξέρω σέ ποιό
σημεῖο βρισκόμαστε σέ νίκη ἤ σέ ἥττα.
Ἄλλωστε ὁ ἑλλανόδικος ἥλιος
μᾶς κρίνει ἀκόμη. Γιατί, ὥς τήν ὥρα,
κανείς ἀπ' τούς δυό μας δέν παραδόθηκε.

THE CONTEST AND THE ADJUDICATOR

I wrestled with fate hand to hand.
He tried to strip me of my face
And I was so badly beaten that,
as I walked, the bones inside me
sounded like broken glass.
At present, I don't know what
point we've reached: victory or defeat.
Besides, the adjudicating sun
is still deciding. For, until now,
neither of us has yielded.

ΤΟ ΜΟΝΟΓΡΑΜΜΑ ΜΟΥ

Τὸ μικρό μου μονόγραμμα στοῦ λινοῦ
παιδικοῦ σακακιοῦ μου τό πέτο: ἀγάπη.

Τὸ μικρό μου μονόγραμμα στοῦ γερον-
τικοῦ μου παλτοῦ τό πέτο: ἀγάπη.

Τὸ μικρό μου μονόγραμμα πάνω
στήν ἐντάφια πλάκα μου: ἀγάπη.

MY MONOGRAM

My tiny monogram on the lapel
of my children's linen jacket: love.

My tiny monogram on the lapel
of my old man's overcoat: love.

My tiny monogram on
my memorial stone: love.

Από τη συλλογή *Χορωδία*

ΠΟΙΗΜΑΤΑ ΓΙΑ ΤΟ ΙΔΙΟ ΒΟΥΝΟ

V
Ἡ οὐράνια δαντέλα,
ἡ σχεδόν κυματίζουσα,
τῶν γραμμῶν σου, θαρρεῖς
ὅταν δύει ὁ ἥλιος
καί γιομίζει ἀγγέλους.

Προχωροῦν, ἀνεβαίνουν
ἀπ' τίς δυό παρυφές
στή μεγάλη κορφή σου.

Συγκεντρώνονται πάνω της
σάν μιά χορωδία.

Ὅσο πού τέλος,
κάποιος ἀπ' ὅλους
ἁπλώνει τό χέρι
κι ἀνάβει τόν ἕσπερο.

From: *Choir*

POEMS FOR THE SAME MOUNTAIN

V
The heavenly lacework,
undulating almost,
of your contours, seems,
when the sun sets,
to fill with angels.

They advance, ascend
on both sides
to your lofty summit.

They assemble upon it
like a choir.

Till in the end,
one of them,
raising an arm,
lights the Hesperus.

ΠΟΙΗΜΑΤΑ ΓΙΑ ΤΟ ΙΔΙΟ ΒΟΥΝΟ

Χ
Παλεύοντας διάσχισα ἀνέμους
πολλούς, πού βρίσκαν τό στῆθος μου
ἀνοιχτό καί μέ πάγωναν. Ὑδρορρόες
κεραυνῶν τό μέτωπό μου, φαγώθηκε,
ἔτσι πού τώρα νά στεκόμαστε
ὁ ἕνας μας ἀντίκρυ στόν ἄλλο,
σάν δυό ἀδελφά γκρίζα
πετρώματα.
  Ἡ γαλήνη σου
ὅμως καί γαλήνη μου πάντοτε.
Καθισμένος στά πόδια σου,
γιομάτος πληγές, μακαρίζω
τήν ὕπαρξη.
  Ἡ μοίρα
μοῦ ἐπέτρεψε ἀπ' ὅλον τόν μέγα
πλοῦτο πού ὑμνῶ, νά ἔχω
κ' ἐγώ στό σύμπαν μιά πέτρα.

POEMS FOR THE SAME MOUNTAIN

    X
Struggling I passed through winds
many winds, that found me with breast
bared and chilled me through. My brow,
gutters for thunderbolts, grew wizened,
so that now we both stand,
each facing the other,
like two twin grey
rocks.
      Your tranquillity
yet ever my tranquillity too.
Sitting at your feet,
covered in wounds, I give praise
to existence.
         Fate
allowed me, of all the great
wealth I laud, to have for myself
a rock in the universe.

ΔΗΜΙΟΥΡΓΙΑ

Λογαριάζω πώς ἔχω νά γράψω ἀκόμη ὥς χίλια ποιήματα. Πάω ν' ἀγοράσω χαρτί γιά ἔξι μέρες. Καί σκέφτομαι: ἄραγε μέ πόσες χιλιάδες ποιήματα νά 'φτιαξε τόν ἥλιο του ὁ Κύριος;

CREATION

I estimate that I still have as many as
a thousand poems to write. I'm off to buy
paper for six days. And I reflect:
with how many thousands of poems
did the Lord create his sun?

Η ΠΟΙΗΣΗ

Ἡ ποίηση εἶναι: ὁ Θεός
πού πορεύεται
πρός ὅλο τόν κόσμο
μέ ἀνοιγμένα τά χέρια του.

POETRY

Poetry is: God
going out to
the whole world
with open arms.

Από τη συλλογή *Ἡ φιλοσοφία τῶν λουλουδιῶν*

Ο ΣΦΥΓΜΟΣ

Τὸ πρωΐ, πρίν ὁ ἥλιος χαμηλώσει ὥς ἐδῶ
κ' ἐνῶ ἀκόμη ἀκουμπᾶ τή χρυσή του
εὐλογία στίς κορφές τῶν βουνῶν,
κατεβαίνω στόν κῆπο. Σκύβω πάνω
ἀπ' τήν ἄσπρη μου τριανταφυλλιά
καί τήν κίτρινη, σκύβω πάνω
ἀπ' τό κόκκινο καί τό ἄσπρο
  γεράνι μου.
 Κι ὅποιον
μίσχο κι ἄν πιάσω (ὡς νά μοῦ ἔχει
τό χέρι του ἁπλώσει ὁ Θεός)
ἀκούω τό σφυγμό του.

From: *The Philosophy of Flowers*

THE PULSE

At daybreak, before the sun reaches down here
and while it's still laying its golden
blessing on the mountaintops,
I go out into the garden. I bend down
beside my white rosebush
the yellow one too, I bend down
beside my red and my white
         geraniums.
         And whichever
stem I take hold of (as if God
has extended his hand to me)
I hear the throb of his pulse.

ΕΠΙΦΑΝΗΣ ΜΑΡΤΥΡΙΑ

Κι ἂν ἀκόμη δέν ἤξερα (ἂν
μοῦ ἦταν ἀόρατος)
Θά μού 'φτανε μόνον
    ἕνα λουλούδι
νά μαντέψω ὅτι κάποιος
    ἥλιος ὑπάρχει
ψηλά στό στερέωμα.

MANIFEST EVIDENCE

Even if I didn't know (if
it were invisible to me),
    one flower
alone would suffice
for me to divine the existence
    of a sun
high in the firmament.

ΕΧΩ ΜΙΛΗΣΕΙ

Ἔχω μιλήσει πολύ στόν ἑαυτό μου,
στούς ἄλλους ὥς καί στά πράγματα.
Μοναχά μέ τό Θεό τόν ἴδιο
δέν ἔτυχε ν' ἀνταλλάξω κουβέντες.
Καί γι' αὐτό κάτι ἐλάχιστο,
ἴσως, θά πρέπει νά γνωρίζει
γιά μένα. Περιορίστηκε σέ ὅσα
τοῦ μετέφεραν τά λουλούδια του.

I'VE SPOKEN

I've spoken a lot with myself,
with others, and even with things.
It was only with God
that I never exchanged a few words.
Which is why, perhaps,
he must know very little
about me. He contented himself with
what his flowers related to him.

ΣΕΜΙΝΑΡΙΟ

Ἄν μέ βλέπαν νά στέκομαι
ὄρθιος, ἀκίνητος, μές
στά λουλούδια μου, ὅπως
αὐτή τή στιγμή,
θά νόμιζαν πώς
τά διδάσκω. Ἐνῶ
εἶμαι ἐγώ πού ἀκούω
κι αὐτά πού μιλοῦν.

Ἔχοντάς με στό μέσο
μοῦ διδάσκουν τό φῶς.

SEMINAR

If anyone saw me standing
upright, motionless, amidst
my flowers, as I am
at this very moment,
he'd think that
I was teaching them. Whereas
it's I who am listening
and they who are speaking.

With me in their midst,
they're teaching me the light.

ΓΕΝΕΣΗ

Αὐτό τό γαρύφαλο, πού κρατώντας το
ἀνάμεσα στά τρία μου δάχτυλα
τό σηκώνω στό φῶς, μοῦ μίλησε καί
παρά τόν κοινό νοῦ μου τό κατανόησα.
Μι' ἁλυσίδα ἀπό ἀτελείωτους γαλαξίες
συνεργάστηκαν, διασταύρωσαν κάτω
στή γῆ φωταψίες – τό σύμπαν ὁλόκληρο
πῆρε μέρος στή γένεση αὐτοῦ τοῦ γαρύφαλου.

Κι αὐτό πού ἀκούω εἶναι οἱ φωνές
τῶν μαστόρων του μέσα του.

CREATION

The carnation that I'm holding
in my three fingers
lifting it up to the light, spoke to me and
despite my simple wits, I understood it.
A chain of interminable galaxies
worked together, flashes of light
intersected on earth – the whole universe
took part in the creation of this carnation.

And what I hear are the voices
of its craftsmen deep inside it.

Από τη συλλογή *Συνάντηση μέ τή θάλασσα*

ΩΣ ΝΑ ΕΠΑΥΕΣ...

Ὡς νά ἔπαυες κάποτε νά εἶσαι νερό,
νά γινόσουνα φῶς ἤ ἀέρας ἤ τίποτα
δέν σέ ἄκουγα πιά. Ἦταν τέτοια
ἡ γαλήνη σου πού νόμιζα πώς
μέ ἄφησες κ' ἔφυγες. Ἀκουγόταν
ἡ μέσα μου ἀδιάκοπη μόνο βοή
πού δέν λάβαινε ἀπόκριση.
Καί μ' ἔπιανε τρόμος
πώς ἔμεινα μόνος μου.

From: *Encounter with the Sea*

AS IF AT TIMES YOU'D CEASED...

As if at times you'd ceased to be water,
becoming light or air or nothing
I would no longer hear you. Your calm
was such that I thought
you'd left me and gone. All that was heard
was the incessant murmur within me
which received no response.
And I was seized by the fear
that I had remained alone.

ΤΟ ΒΛΕΜΜΑ ΜΟΥ...

Τό βλέμμα μου ὑπῆρξε ὁ καθρέφτης σου,
θάλασσα. Μέσα του ἐφάνη τό ὑδάτινο
σῶμα σου. Ἐσύ δέν ἐγνώριζες τή μορφή,
τή βοή, τίς πότε λαμπρές καί τίς πότε
ταραγμένες μεταμορφώσεις σου.
Καθώς κι ὁ ὡραῖος γείτονάς σου
ὁ Ταΰγετος. Ἀκόμη κι ὁ ἥλιος.
Αὐτή τή στιγμή μᾶς φωτίζει
τοῦ σύμπαντος ὁ μέγας τυφλός.

Σέ μένα ἡ χάρη καί ἡ τιμή
καί ἡ δόξα. Γιατί ὅλα ὑπήρχατε
δίχως νά γνωρίζετε πώς ὑπάρχετε,
θάλασσα. Ἡ βεβαίωση ἔγινε
μέσα στό βλέμμα μου.

MY GAZE…

My gaze was your mirror,
dear sea. In it appeared your aqueous
body. You never knew your form,
your roar, your sometimes radiant
sometimes turbulent transformations.
Just like your splendid neighbour
Taygetos. Like the sun too.
Shining on us at this very moment
is the blind giant of the universe.

Mine is the fortune, the honour
and the glory. For all of you existed
without knowing that you exist,
dear sea. The confirmation came
in my gaze.

ΤΟ ΜΟΝΙΜΟ ΟΝΕΙΡΟ...

Τό μόνιμο ὄνειρο τῆς ζωῆς μου τό εἶδα
δίπλα σου, θάλασσα: Φωταγωγήθηκε
ἡ ἄβυσσο μέσα στόν ἄνθρωπο.
Πώς ἔσμιξαν κ' ἔγιναν ἕνα χρῶμα
τά χρώματα τῶν διαφόρων φυλῶν.
Καί πήρανε ὅλοι τήν ἴδια ὁδό.
Κ' ἡ ὁδός ὁδηγοῦσε σέ σημεῖο
ἀπ' ὅπου κάτι θ' ἀνάτελλε. Κ' εἶδα
τόν ἕνα ἄνθρωπο ἔπειτα
νά πατάει στό νερό καί νά στέκεται
ὄρθιος.
    Κ' εἶδα μετά
νά ἐγκαταλείπουνε τ' ἄστρα
τίς θέσεις τους ἄξαφνα κι ὅλα
μαζί, νά φέρνουνε κύκλους γύρω
ἀπ' τόν ἄνθρωπο, πού βάδιζε (ἐνώπιος
ἐνωπίω μέ τό ἄπειρο) πανύψηλος
πάνω σου.
    (Καί ψιθύρισα
μέσα μου στόν πρῶτο τυχαῖο
ἄγνωστο πού συνάντησα στόν κόσμο
μετά: «Φίλε, σέ ξέρω, σέ εἶδα
πού βάδιζες πάνω στή θάλασσα.»).

THE CONSTANT DREAM...

The constant dream of my life came to me,
dear sea, beside you: the abyss within man
was flooded with light.
The colours of the various races
merged, became one colour.
And all followed the same path.
And the path led to a point
where something was about to dawn. Then
I saw the one man
walking on water and standing
upright.
    And next I saw
the stars suddenly leaving
their positions and all of them
together forming circles around
the man, who was walking (face to face
with the infinite), toweringly tall,
upon you.
    (And I whispered
under my breath to the first
stranger I next chanced to meet
in the world: "Friend, I know you,
I saw you walking on the sea.").

ΕΙΧΑ ΠΑΕΙ...

Εἶχα πάει σ' ἕναν κόσμο πού μοῦ θύμιζε
τίς σκοτεινότερες ὧρες σου – ὅταν
χωρισμένη σέ κύματα, πήγαινες,
γύριζες, βάδιζες ὄρθια σχεδόν
μές στόν ὁρίζοντα, σχηματίζοντας
ἕνα θαμπό παραπέτασμα,
πού πίσω του ἔκανε μεγάλη προσπάθεια
ν' ἀνατείλει ὁ ἥλιος – ὅπως κ' ἐγώ,
πού δέν ἤμουν ἥλιος, δέν ἤμουν
ἄστρο, ἀλλά ἕνα ἔντομο ἁπλῶς
φωτεινό, πού παγίδεψε
ὁ κόσμος μές στήν ἀράχνη του.

I'D GONE...

I'd gone into a world that reminded me
of your darkest hours – when
divided into waves, you'd go,
return, stride almost erect
into the horizon, forming
an opaque screen,
behind which the sun made
a great effort to rise – as did I,
who was no sun, no
star, merely a luminous
insect caught up
in the world's web.

ΑΛΛΑ ΚΥΜΑΤΑ...

Ἄλλα κύματα μέσα μου σκαμπανέβαζαν,
βούλιαζαν τήν κιβωτό μέ τό λόγο.
Βρισκόμουν σέ ἀδιάκοπη ἀμάχη
γιά τό κρίθινό μου ψωμί καί μαζί
γιά τά δάκρυα τοῦ ἀδελφοῦ μου
Ἰησοῦ, πού πολλά ἀπ' αὐτά
θά σοῦ ἔφεραν τά ποτάμια σου.
Ἀλλά ποῦ νά τά βρεῖς! Ἔτσι
ἀσίγαστη πού εἶσαι,
οἱ σταγόνες τους, θάλασσα,
(μιά δεύτερη θάλασσα)
μπερδευτῆκαν μέ τίς σταγόνες σου.

OTHER WAVES...

Other waves within me tossed,
sank the ark with the word.
I found myself in a constant struggle
for my barley bread and together
for the tears of my brother
Jesus, so many of which
your rivers must have borne to you.
Yet how are you to find them! For
restless as you are,
dear sea, these droplets
(a second sea)
mingled with your own.

ΠΟΛΥ ΔΙΑΛΟΓΙΣΤΗΚΑ...

Πολύ διαλογίστηκα δίπλα σου, θάλασσα. Όσο πού ἀρκέστηκα μόνο νά βλέπω τό γύρω μου φῶς. Ἕνα κουβάρι σοφίας ἡ σταγόνα σου. Ἕνα κουβάρι σοφίας ἡ ζωή. Ἕνα κουβάρι σοφίας τό σύμπαν, πού δέν ξεδιπλώνεται.

I PONDERED MUCH…

I pondered much beside you, dear sea.
Till I was content simply to regard
the light around me. One droplet
of yours is a clew of wisdom. Life
is a clew of wisdom. The universe is
a clew of wisdom that can't be unravelled.

Η ΠΟΙΗΣΗ...

Ὅ,τι μπόρεσα νά διασώσω
(στόν κόσμο πού πῆγα)
τό διέσωσα, θάλασσα.

Ἡ ψυχή μου ἕνα σμῆνος
μυριάδων πουλιῶν
πού τ' ἀλώνιζε ἡ θύελλα.

Ὅσα διασώθηκαν
βρῆκαν τό δέντρο τους.

Φτερούγισαν κ' ἔμειναν
μέσα στίς λέξεις.

POETRY...

Whatever I was able to save
(in the world I went into)
I saved, dear sea.

My soul was a flock
of countless birds
racked by the storm.

Those that were saved
found their tree.

They fluttered and remained
inside my words.

ΔΙΠΛΑ ΣΤ' ΑΛΛΑ...

Δίπλα στ' ἄλλα βιβλία μου, ἀόρατος,
βέβαιος ὅμως, κ' ἕνας τόμος σιωπῆς.
Σ' αὐτόν περιέχονται ὅλα ὅσα
ἔκρυψα κι ὅσα δέν πρόφτασαν
νά κάνουν τή μέσα μου μακριά
διαδρομή νά βγοῦνε στό φῶς.
Οἱ σελίδες τεράστιες, τό βάρος του
ἀσήκωτο. Δέν θά τόν διαβάσει
κανείς. Θά τόν πάρει ὅπως
εἶναι ὁ Θεός νά τόν βάλει
στήν οὐράνια βιβλιοθήκη του.

BESIDE MY OTHER...

Beside my other books, invisible,
existent nonetheless, is a volume of silence.
Contained in it are all the things
I hid from view and all that failed
to make the long journey within
me and emerge into the light.
Too weighty to lift, its pages
huge. No one will ever
read it. God will take it just
as it is and place it
on his celestial bookshelves.

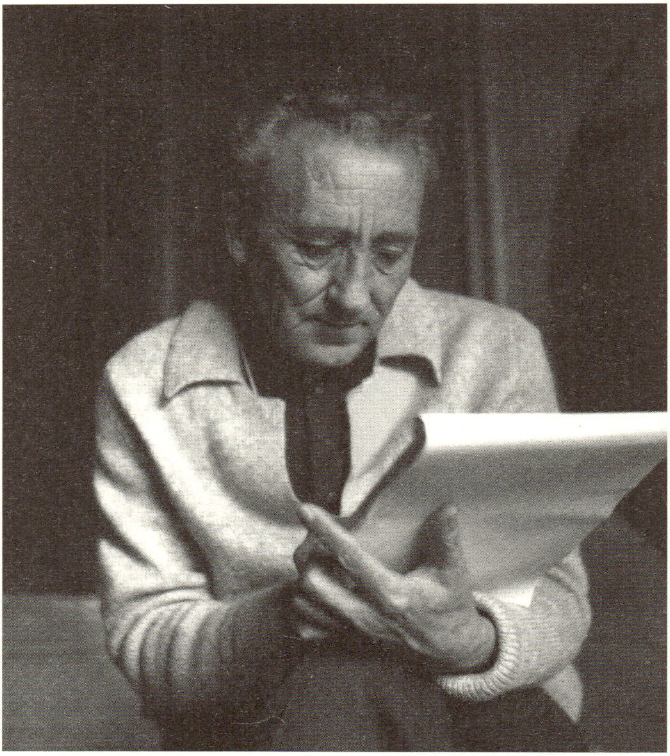

Chronology

1912	He is born in Krokees in Laconia on January 1st (December 19th, 1911 according to the Julian Calendar).
1917	September 20th. He enters the first class of Primary School in Krokees. His family is obliged to move there from their home in Ploumitsa.
1924	September 15th. He enters the first class of High School in Gytheion.
1929	November. He moves to Athens to continue his studies, but is unable to because of financial hardship. He publishes his first collection *Under Shadows and Lights*.
1934	He meets Calliope Apostolidi, a university student. They work together as clerks in the Army General Stores in Piraeus. They marry on August 20th.
1936	Their daughter, Jenny, is born on April 9th. His book, *The War*, is burned by the August 4th Regime as being subversive.
1938	Their son Kostas is born on July 9th. Vrettakos finds employment as a clerk in the Ministry of Works.
1940	He is called up to the army during the Albanian Cam-

paign and fights in the front line. He is awarded the State Prize for Poetry.

1941 April 14th. The Regiment in which he is serving is wiped out and he returns to Athens on foot.

1942-44 He takes an active part in the National Resistance and joins the Greek Communist Party.

1945 He is awarded the National Resistance Prize for his poems of resistance.

1948 He is expelled from the Greek Communist Party following the publication of his prose work *Two Men Talk of Peace in the World*. He is forced to move to Piraeus, where he eventually finds work as a customs official. He meets the poet Angelos Sikelianos and they remain friends till the latter's death.

1955 He is elected a City Counsellor in Piraeus and is extremely active as Chairman of the City's Arts Committee.

1956 He is awarded the State Prize for Poetry for the second time.

1957 He visits the Soviet Union as part of the World Meeting of Democratic Youth.

1962 He moves back to Athens with his family.

1964 He works as an attendant in the vestiary of the National Theatre. He travels to Bucharest and Venice and the Dalmatian Coast.

1967 His son is arrested and imprisoned by the Military Junta. Nikiforos goes into self-imposed exile, leaving for the Swiss Alps, where finds refuge in the Pestalozzi International Children's Village.

1970	He settles in Palermo in Sicily following a proposal by Bruno Lavagnini, President of the Sicilian Institute for Byzantine and Modern Greek Studies, to work on the compilation of an Italian-Greek dictionary.
1974	He suffers a severe form of tuberculosis and is hospitalized for almost six months in a clinic in Palermo before being sent to convalesce in Serres in the French Alps. He returns to Greece on August 16th following the fall of the Military Junta.
1976	He receives the Ouranis Award from the Academy of Athens for his books *The River Buech and the Seven Elegies* and *Ode to the Sun*.
1978	He resides in his ancestral home in Ploumitsa.
1980	He is proposed, together with Yannis Ritsos, for the Nobel Prize for Literature. He is awarded the Belgian Knoken International Prize.
1981	He is awarded the Asla Prize by the Society of Sicilian Arts and Letters.
1982	He is awarded the State Prize for Poetry for the third time for his work *Liturgy Below the Acropolis*.
1985	March 22nd. He is awarded the Excellence in Letters Prize by the Academy of Athens.
1987	February 26th. He is elected to the Academy of Athens.
1988	February 9th. He is officially instated in the Academy of Athens. The topic of his maiden speech: "Poetic Discourse and National Truth".
1989	He is again proposed, together with Yannis Ritsos, for the Nobel Prize for Literature.

1990   He is awarded the Bulgarian Vaptsarov International Prize.

1991   May 31st. He is awarded an Honorary Doctorate by the University of Athens. He is proposed for the fourth time for the Nobel Prize for Literature. June 20th, *Liturgy Below the Acropolis* is performed on Mt. Taygetus with the poet himself reading the Epilogue. August 4th, he dies in Ploumitsa.

Translated from the Chronology compiled by Georgia Kakourou-Chroni.

Book-length English Translations

Thirty Years in the Rain. The Selected Poetry of Nikiforos Vrettakos, Translated by Robert Zaller and Lili Bita, Boston: Somerset Hall Press 2005.

Gifts in Abeyance. Last Poems 1981-91, Translated from the Modern Greek with an Introduction by David Connolly, Minneapolis: Nostos Books 1992.

Η Φιλοσοφία των Λουλουδιών / The Philosophy of Flowers, Translated by David Connolly, Illustrated by George Varlamos, Athens: Artigraf 1990.

Index of Greek Titles

Ἄλλα κύματα... 92
Ἀπολογισμός 26
Ἀπόλογος σ' ἕνα βουνό 28
Γένεση 82
Δενδροφύτευση 54
Δημιουργία 70
Δίπλα στ' ἄλλα... 98
Εἶχα πάει... 90
Ἕνα ἄσμα γιά τή γῆ 46
Ἐπιφανής Μαρτυρία 76
Ἔχω μιλήσει 78
Ἡ γραφή μου 34
Ἡ ἰδέα τῆς ἐξόδου 56
Ἡ καταστροφή τῶν προσώπων 60
Ἡ κιβωτός 58
Ἡ μεταμόρφωση τοῦ τοπίου 36
Ἡ μετάφραση 38
Ἡ πάλη καί ὁ ἑλλανόδικος 62
Ἡ ποίηση 72
Ἡ ποίηση... 96

Ή φιλοξενία 40
Ματαιοδοξία 24
Μετάγγιση 42
Μικρή ώδή 48
Ό άγρός τῶν λέξεων 52
Ό ἄλλος στρατιώτης 50
Ό σφυγμός 74
Ὅ,τι καί νά συμβεῖ 44
Ποιήματα για το ίδιο βουνό V 66
Ποιήματα για το ίδιο βουνό X 68
Πολύ διαλογίστηκα... 94
Σεμινάριο 80
Τό βλέμμα μου 86
Τό δύσκολο ὄρος 32
Τό μεγάλο ἔργο 30
Τό μόνιμο ὄνειρο 88
Τό μονόγραμμά μου 64
Ώς νά ἔπαυες... 84

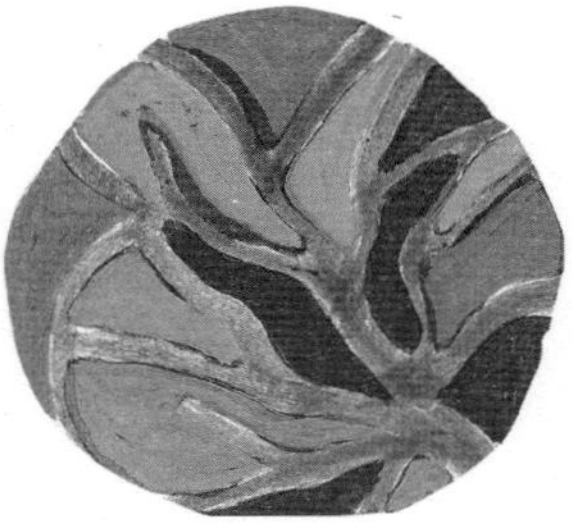

READ THE **MODERN GREEK CLASSICS**

C.P. CAVAFY
Selected Poems
Translated by David Connolly

ODYSSEUS ELYTIS
In the Name of Luminosity and Transparency
Introduction by Dimitris Daskalopoulos

ANDREAS LASKARATOS
Reflexions
Translated by Simon Darragh

ALEXANDROS PAPADIAMANDIS
Fey Folk
Translated by David Connolly

GEORGE SEFERIS
Novel and Other Poems
Translated by Roderick Beaton

GEORGIOS VIZYENOS
Thracian Tales
Translated by Peter Mackridge

GEORGIOS VIZYENOS
Moskov Selim
Translated by Peter Mackridge

Rebetika
Songs from the Old Greek Underworld
Translated by Katharine Butterworth & Sara Schneider

www.aiora.gr